MARKET LEADER

Test File

PRE-INTERMEDIATE
BUSINESS ENGLISH

Christine Johnson

LTS Training and Consulting

Longman

FINANCIAL TIMES
World business newspaper.

Pearson Education Limited
Edinburgh Gate
Harlow
Essex CM20 2JE
England

First published 2002

ISBN 0 582 506964

Second impression 2003

Set in 10.5/12.5pt Meta Plus

Printed in Spain by Mateu Cromo, S.A. Pinto, Madrid

www.market-leader.net

Acknowledgements
We are grateful to the following for permission to reproduce copyright material:
Financial Times Limited for an extract adapted from 'Saint Laurent wraps up haute couture career' by Jo Johnson published in the *Financial Times* 8th January 2002; Guardian Newspapers Limited for an extract adapted from 'Three simple steps to a 4-day week' by Barbara Oaff published in the *Guardian* 26th January 2002 © Barbara Oaff 2002; and Kyodo News International, Inc., for an extract adapted from 'Hear the stroke engine purr' by Kakumi Kobayashi published in Japan Today 31st December 2001.

Project managed by Chris Hartley

Contents

Entry Test

You are going to hear a conversation between three people: Ruth, Irena and Bob. Before you listen, read the first five questions. Then listen and mark your answers. Choose the best answer: a, b or c.

EXAMPLE:

The conversation takes place in …

- ☐ **a)** London.
- ✓ **b)** Luton.
- ☐ **c)** Latvia.

1 The meeting takes place …
- ☐ **a)** at the airport.
- ☐ **b)** in the company's offices.
- ☐ **c)** in a restaurant.

2 Which person is the visitor?
- ☐ **a)** Ruth
- ☐ **b)** Irena
- ☐ **c)** Bob

3 Which person is an assistant?
- ☐ **a)** Ruth
- ☐ **b)** Irena
- ☐ **c)** Bob

4 Which person hasn't met Bob before?
- ☐ **a)** Ruth
- ☐ **b)** Irena
- ☐ **c)** They have both met Bob before.

5 Which person sent a message this morning?
- ☐ **a)** Ruth
- ☐ **b)** Irena
- ☐ **c)** Bob

Now read the next five questions. Listen again and then mark your answers.

6 Irena says that her journey was …
- ☐ **a)** good.
- ☐ **b)** not so bad.
- ☐ **c)** terrible.

7 Irena says she is sorry because …
- ☐ **a)** she went to the wrong office.
- ☐ **b)** she forgot something important.
- ☐ **c)** she didn't arrive on time.

8 The plane was delayed because of …
- [ ] **a)** the weather.
- [ ] **b)** security problems.
- [ ] **c)** a mechanical problem.

9 Ruth's office is on the ………… floor.
- [ ] **a)** 1st
- [ ] **b)** 4th
- [ ] **c)** 5th

10 Bob offers …
- [ ] **a)** to carry Irena's bags.
- [ ] **b)** to take Irena's coat.
- [ ] **c)** to bring Irena a cup of coffee.

Vocabulary

A **Mark the word that doesn't belong in each group.**

EXAMPLE:

| **a)** car | **b)** plane | **c)** ~~airport~~ | **d)** train | **e)** truck |

11 a) sales	**b)** marketing	**c)** finance	**d)** manager	**e)** personnel
12 a) engineer	**b)** visitor	**c)** secretary	**d)** receptionist	**e)** accountant
13 a) company	**b)** department	**c)** head office	**d)** subsidiary	**e)** meeting
14 a) voice mail	**b)** e-mail	**c)** report	**d)** letter	**e)** memo
15 a) client	**b)** colleague	**c)** assistant	**d)** manager	**e)** team member

B **Choose a word from the box which has a similar meaning.**

EXAMPLE: telephone – **c)** *call*

a) journey	**b)** profit	**c)** ~~call~~	**d)** pay
e) buy	**f)** invoice	**g)** client	**h)** employment

16 bill …………

17 trip …………

18 salary …………

19 job …………

20 customer …………

C **Mark the verb that does <u>not</u> go with the noun.**

EXAMPLE:

a) send	**b)** receive	**c)** pay	**d)** ~~make~~	an invoice
21 a) drive	**b)** attend	**c)** lead	**d)** arrange	a meeting
22 a) finish	**b)** read	**c)** write	**d)** pay	the report
23 a) make	**b)** receive	**c)** solve	**d)** have	a phone call
24 a) enjoy	**b)** spend	**c)** start	**d)** leave	your job
25 a) spend	**b)** make	**c)** lose	**d)** attend	money

D **Choose the best answer to complete each sentence.**

26 When a salesperson wants to visit a client, he or she normally telephones a week or two before to make …

a) a message.　**b)** an appointment.　**c)** an engagement.　**d)** a reservation.

27 When you arrange to meet someone, it is a good idea to send an e-mail to ………… the date and time of your meeting.

a) cancel　　　**b)** order　　　**c)** place　　　**d)** confirm

28 When you are a visitor and you arrive at a company, you should go first to …

a) Deliveries.　**b)** the restaurant　**c)** Reception　**d)** the mail room.

29 Sales staff sometimes ………… their important customers at a restaurant.

a) entertain　　**b)** employ　　**c)** estimate　　**d)** enjoy

30 If you want to go to a popular restaurant, you should telephone first to ………… a table.

a) fix　　　　**b)** recommend　　**c)** reserve　　**d)** order

Grammar

A **Choose the best word or phrase from the box to complete the text.**

a) the cheapest	**e)** slowest
b) faster	**f)** as
c) more	**g)** than
d) less	**h)** ~~better~~

If you have a long distance to travel, and money is not a problem, then it is
..*better*... to go by plane, because it is ………… ³¹ and ………… ³²
convenient. Travelling by bus is ………… ³³ but also the ………… ³⁴ form of
transport. Trains are usually more expensive ………… ³⁵ buses.

B **Write the past simple form of each verb to complete the text.**

Bill Gates (write) .*wrote*. his first computer program at the age of 13. He
(spend) ………… ³⁶ a lot of time using computers. But at that time
computers were expensive: it (cost) ………… ³⁷ $40 an hour to use one. Bill
(work) ………… ³⁸ during his school holidays. That way, he (make)
………… ³⁹ some money, and he also (learn) ………… ⁴⁰ a lot about using
computers.

C **Choose the best word or phrase to complete the text.**

Ben Driver and Sheila Quirke both ..*work*.. for AAA, the Australian Advertising
Agency. But they .... [41] know each other. Ben .... [42] based
in Sydney and .... [43] a lot in his work. Sheila .... [44] the
company's headquarters in Melbourne and .... [45] travel much.
John Fowles, ... [46] Managing Director, thinks highly of both of
.... [47] . The Agency .... [48] open a new office in Perth, and
John is planning to appoint either Ben or Sheila as the Manager.
Sheila .... [49] more management experience, but Ben is excellent at
client relations. What .... [50] John do?

EXAMPLE:

	a) ~~work~~	**b)** works	**c)** is working	**d)** worked
41	**a)** aren't	**b)** doesn't	**c)** don't	**d)** not
42	**a)** am	**b)** is	**c)** are	**d)** he's
43	**a)** travels	**b)** travel	**c)** travelling	**d)** are travelling
44	**a)** work at	**b)** works at	**c)** work for	**d)** works for
45	**a)** aren't	**b)** isn't	**c)** don't	**d)** doesn't
46	**a)** they	**b)** there	**c)** their	**d)** they're
47	**a)** they	**b)** them	**c)** their	**d)** him
48	**a)** going	**b)** going to	**c)** is going to	**d)** be going to
49	**a)** is having	**b)** had	**c)** have	**d)** has
50	**a)** can	**b)** may	**c)** should	**d)** need

D **Cross out the extra word to form a correct question.**

EXAMPLE: Do you ~~do~~ speak French?

51 How many people do work for your company?

52 Is it is a manufacturing company?

53 Do can you describe some of your products?

54 Are these products are yours?

55 Where to do you export to?

Reading **A** Read the article and answer the questions below.

A young boy and his mother were shopping in the toy section in Takashimaya Co's store in Tokyo right before Christmas. On display was a robot cat that looked and moved just like a living
5 animal. 'It's so real, Mum,' the boy cried as he watched the cat.

'Excellent. We should take this,' said the boy's mother, 26-year-old Junko Shibata, who seemed happy to pay ¥185,000 (nearly US$1,500) for the
10 toy.

The cat, which has 15 electric motors inside it, sounds like a real cat, moves its body and responds to the people around it.

Omron Corp, a major Japanese maker of
15 robots and automated equipment, has decided to start developing digital animals as toys. The firm launched the new cat in November.

'Our robot cat may be too pricey, but this is our first product in the market of robot pets. We
20 want to find out who really wants our product,' said Toshihiro Tashima, who leads Omron's project on electric pets.

At the toy shop in Tokyo, most visitors said they would like to bring home such toys, and
25 hope that prices will drop.

A report says that by 2010 personal robots will have a 50.2% market share of the entire Japanese robot market. This will be almost double the share for robots for industrial use (28.4%). The
30 boom of various robots for personal and family use in Japan started in 1999 when Sony Corp launched its popular series of Aibo robot pets.

The market has since grown steadily with newcomers such as a man-like robot that can
35 walk down the stairs and electric fish that can swim.

From *Japan Today*
reprinted in the *Guardian*

Choose the best answer to each question.

56 The article is mainly about ...

    a) robot animals.

    b) robots for use in industry.

    c) Christmas shopping in Tokyo.

    d) The Japanese electronics industry.

57 The robot cat is ...

    a) a computer game.

    b) a live animal.

    c) equipment for use in the house.

    d) a toy.

58 The robot cat is ...

    a) very expensive.

    b) quite expensive.

    c) medium-priced.

    d) low-priced.

59 The robot cat is produced by ...

    a) Takashimaya Co.

    b) Omron Corp.

    c) Sony Corp.

    d) The manufacturer's name is not in the article.

60 Which is true?

    a) The robot cat is a new product.

    b) The robot cat has been on the market since 1999.

    c) The company that makes the cat knows a lot about the market for this product.

    d) The company already makes other robot animals.

61 Most visitors to the store ...
    a) loved the cat.
    b) were happy with the price.
    c) thought that the cat was not very real.
    d) didn't like the cat.

62 The market share for personal robots in Japan ...
    a) is not growing at the moment.
    b) will not increase very much.
    c) will be much bigger than the market share for industrial robots by 2010.
    d) will be twice as big by 2010.

63 The meaning of *pricey* (line 18) is ...
    a) cheap.
    b) high-priced.
    c) has no fixed price.
    d) difficult to price.

64 The meaning of *boom* (line 30) is ...
    a) a rapid increase in sales.
    b) a sharp fall in sales.
    c) a slow rise in sales.
    d) a steady fall in sales.

65 The meaning of *newcomers* (line 34) in this article is ...
    a) new types of business.
    b) new customers.
    c) new trends in the market.
    d) products that are new on the market.

Progress Test 1 (Units 1–4)

Nelson Ferreira works for an aircraft manufacturer. He is making a presentation to some people who are interested in buying aircraft.

Read the first three questions. Then listen and mark your answers.

1 The part of the presentation which you hear is …
   a) the introduction.
   b) some basic facts that come before the main part.
   c) the main part.
   d) the conclusion.

2 The company is …
   a) a state-owned company.
   b) a family-owned company.
   c) a multinational company.
   d) a company which has shares traded on the stock exchange.

3 The customers are mainly interested in …
   a) an executive jet plane.
   b) military aircraft.
   c) commercial aircraft.
   d) aircraft in general.

Now read the next seven questions. Then listen again and write in your answers.

4 The country where the company is based: ....

5 The year when the company was set up: ....

6 In 1994, it was:
   a) sold.   b) merged with another manufacturer.
   c) privatised.   d) reorganised.

7 Gross revenue last year: $..........................

8 Net earnings last year: $..........................

9 Number of employees at present: ....

10 In the last five years, the company has:
   a) grown a lot.
   b) grown a little.
   c) stayed the same size.
   d) become smaller.

Vocabulary

A **Mark the word that doesn't belong in each group.**

EXAMPLE:

a) plane	**b)** train	**c)** car	**d)** ~~airport~~	**e)** truck
11 a) ambitious	**b)** energetic	**c)** enthusiastic	**d)** experience	**e)** smart
12 a) profit	**b)** loss	**c)** revenues	**d)** growth	**e)** earnings
13 a) hire	**b)** resign	**c)** dismiss	**d)** retire	**e)** sack
14 a) purchase	**b)** deliver	**c)** dispatch	**d)** return	**e)** warehouse
15 a) difficult	**b)** poor	**c)** unsatisfactory	**d)** successful	**e)** disappointing

B **Match each verb with the noun that goes with it.**

EXAMPLE: serve – **b)** *customers*

16 boost	**a)** a need
17 run	**b)** ~~customers~~
18 meet	**c)** sales
19 save	**d)** goods
20 earn	**e)** a bonus
	f) a business
	g) opportunities
	h) time

C **Choose the best answer.**

21 A credit card can no longer be used after the ...
   a) latest date.
   b) retirement date.
   c) payment date.
   d) expiry date.

22 If you return goods to the seller because you were dissatisfied with them, you get ...
   a) a retail
   b) a refund
   c) a discount
   d) a revenue

23 What do you say if you don't have a particular product available to sell? 'Sorry, we are ...
   a) out of stock.'
   b) out of order.'
   c) ex-warehouse.'
   d) unreliable.'

24 If you want to leave your job, you usually have .... of one to three months.
   a) a leaving schedule
   b) a notice period
   c) time off
   d) early retirement

25 Someone who enjoys meeting and talking to new people is ...
  a) outdoing.
  b) outspoken.
  c) outgoing.
  d) outflowing.

26 All the people who work in a particular company or factory are called ...
  a) workmates.
  b) working capital.
  c) the working group.
  d) the workforce.

27 When a company offers shares for sale on the stock exchange for the first time, we say it ...
  a) markets shares.
  b) sells stock.
  c) goes public.
  d) sets up.

28 If you have tried to solve a problem without success for a long time, but at last you find a way, you make ...
  a) a break-up.
  b) a breakthrough.
  c) a breakdown.
  d) a break-out.

29 If you want to make sure that the environment is not harmed or damaged, you try to .... it.
  a) exploit
  b) enhance
  c) extend
  d) protect

30 If you have a business plan and you need money to develop your idea, you have to ...
  a) make an investigation.
  b) raise investment.
  c) make an invention.
  d) extend invitations.

Functions

Choose the most polite response.

31 You make a phone call to Pat King. Her secretary answers. You say:
  a) I want to speak to Pat King.
  b) Pat King, please.
  c) I'd like to speak to Pat King, please.
  d) I can't get through to Pat King.

32 On the phone, the caller says something you didn't understand. You say:
  a) Sorry, I didn't catch that.
  b) You're not speaking clearly.
  c) I don't understand.
  d) What?

33 You answer the phone in your office. The caller wants to speak to your colleague, who isn't in the office today. You say:

a) She's not here.

b) Sorry. She can't talk to you today.

c) You can't speak to her. You can speak to me.

d) I'm afraid she isn't in today. Can I take a message?

34 You are the seller in a negotiation. The buyer needs the goods next week, but your delivery time is ten days. You say:

a) No – that's too difficult.

b) That's impossible. Our delivery time is ten days.

c) Next week!!

d) I'm afraid we can't deliver next week, but we could deliver in ten days.

35 In a meeting about a project, someone says: 'I think we should cancel the project.'

You disagree:

a) You are wrong!

b) I disagree completely – that's a stupid idea.

c) But this is an important project for us, and it's going to make a lot of money!

d) You're crazy!

Grammar

A Present tenses

Complete this extract from a CEO's speech about his company. Write the verb in the correct tense: present simple or present continuous.

'As you know, our company (grow) .... [36] rapidly at present. We (employ) .... [37] 10 percent more staff than we did last year, and we (recruit) .... [38] more staff all the time. We also (produce) .... [39] 150 machines per month – that's an increase of 15 percent since last year. We (develop) .... [40] a new model of the Turbomaster at the moment, which we think will be a big success. We (know) .... [41] our markets well. Our customers (like) .... [42] our existing products, and we feel confident that they will like the improvements we have made in the new design. We (launch) .... [43] the new model next May, in time for the Munich Trade Fair.'

B Past tenses

Complete the story. Write the verbs in the correct tense: past simple or past continuous.

Catherine (have) .... [44] a busy day at work yesterday. She (try) .... [45] all morning to negotiate a deal worth $90,000 with BAB, an important new customer. But the BAB buyer (demand) .... [46] immediate delivery. Catherine's company (not have) .... [47] enough goods in stock to meet the order so quickly. She (telephone) .... [48] to several different warehouses, but none of them (can) .... [49] supply the goods in time. Then, at 4 p.m. – just when Catherine (lose) .... [50] hope of getting the deal – her telephone (ring) .... [51]. It was John, one of her colleagues from the sales department. He (tell) .... [52] her that CCI, an existing customer, (have) .... [53] problems with the computer system in their warehouse, and they (want) .... [54] to postpone delivery of a big order scheduled for the next day. So Catherine was able to send the CCI delivery to BAB instead and close the deal! Catherine's manager (praise) .... [55] her for her hard work and creativity.

C Modals

Read the information about regulations for using an electric bicycle. Then complete the sentences below with an appropriate modal verb from the list. Use each modal verb once only.

Regulations regarding the use of electric bicycles:	
Driving licence?	NO
Helmet?	YES
Maximum speed?	30km/hour
Insurance?	Recommended
Use cycle paths?	YES
Use roads?	YES

a) must   **b)** mustn't   **c)** can

d) should   **e)** shouldn't   **f)** don't have to / don't need to

To ride an electric bicycle ...

56 You .... have a driving licence.

57 You .... wear a helmet on your head.

58 You .... drive at more than 30 kilometres an hour.

59 Insurance is not necessary, but it's a good idea: you .... have it!

60 You .... ride on both cycle paths and on the road.

Reading

Read the article and answer the questions.

James Dyson, millionaire inventor and successful British businessman, has surprised his country by deciding to move production to the Far East.

The 54-year-old design engineer is well-known for his invention of a powerful vacuum cleaner that operates without a bag. Dyson spent 15 years trying to persuade the banks to support his ideas and enable him to set up production of the new vacuum cleaners. Now, after six years in business, his factory in a small town in the west of England produces 8,000 vacuum cleaners a day. Moving the main production facility to Malaysia will result in a loss of 800 jobs. Both the UK government and the unions have expressed their horror at the decision.

The company, which employs 1,800 people in total, said it had decided to move production because of the success of a plant it established in Malaysia two years ago. Labour costs at the Malaysian plant are only £1.50 an hour: in the UK they are £4.10 an hour. But the quality of the Malaysian cleaners is as high as the British-made ones.

A number of other companies have also moved production to lower cost countries in recent months. Many people fear for the future of British manufacturing if this trend continues.

Dyson believes the move will enable the company to cut production costs by 30 percent. He plans to put the savings into research and development in a drive to create new technology products for the future. The R&D department will continue to be based in Britain.

The company achieved sales of £220 million in 2000 and spends around 10 percent of turnover on new product development. Dyson described R&D as the 'heart and soul' of the business. He said the decision to cut back the UK workforce was a sad and difficult one.

From the Guardian

61 James Dyson ...

    a) has been in business for a long time.

    b) started his business with his own money.

    c) developed a new product.

    d) has a factory in London.

62 Dyson's product ...

    a) is a new technology product.

    b) sells only in Britain.

    c) was first produced 15 years ago.

    d) sells only in the Far East.

63 Dyson wants to move the production to Malaysia because ...

    a) his main markets are in the Far East.

    b) production is cheaper than in the UK.

    c) he lives there.

    d) many other British companies are based there.

64 Dyson's move will enable him to ...

    a) keep some production in the UK.

    b) have his R&D department in Malaysia.

    c) put more money into R&D.

    d) reduce the cost of R&D.

65 Dyson's decision has 'surprised his country'. That means the British people ...

    a) think it is a good idea.

    b) expected this decision.

    c) didn't expect this decision.

    d) don't think it will make a big difference to British manufacturing.

66 The company ...

    a) has a factory in Malaysia now.

    b) has no experience of manufacturing in Malaysia.

    c) tried to move to Malaysia two years ago but was not successful.

    d) had a factory in Malaysia for two years, then closed it.

67 Dyson wants to spend more money on ...

    a) research and development.

    b) selling.

    c) better production facilities.

    d) his staff.

68 How much did Dyson spend on R&D in the year 2000?

    a) £200,000

    b) £2.2 million

    c) £22 million

    d) £220 million

69 How does Dyson feel about moving to Malaysia?

    a) He's completely happy about it.

    b) He is sorry that people will lose their jobs.

    c) He isn't sure about the decision at the moment.

    d) He wants to live in Malaysia.

70 Dyson says that R&D is the 'heart and soul' of the business. He means …

    a) it is the most difficult part.

    b) it is the most important part.

    c) it is the most expensive part.

    d) it is the most interesting part.

Writing

You were one of the people who attended Nelson Ferreira's presentation (in the Listening Test).

Below are some details of an aircraft made by Nelson's company. Your company wants to buy corporate aircraft, and you think this is the aircraft they should choose. Complete the memo using the information.

Write about 50 to 60 words.

Features:

		Cost:
large size	excellent performance	medium-priced
comfortable	reliable	low running costs
safe	good after-sales service contract	

Memo

To: The CEO

From: The purchasing team

Date: 5 May 200-

Re: Purchase of aircraft for company use

We have looked at several models of aircraft which could be suitable for our company and we would like to recommend the Ambassador, which is manufactured in Brazil by BrazAir Corporation.

This aircraft has several advantages …

We attach a detailed report.

Progress Test 2 (Units 5–8)

You are going to hear part of a meeting between four people who all work in the same unit: Max is head of the unit and is the chairperson, Jack is a project leader, Patricia is client relations manager and Maria is finance manager.

Read the first three questions. Then listen and mark your answers.

1 The main topic that the people in the meeting have to discuss is ...
   a) how to cut down running costs.
   b) how to motivate staff.
   c) how to sell services effectively.

2 Jack's suggestion is ...
   a) to organise a dinner at a restaurant for all staff.
   b) to invite new customers to expensive restaurants.
   c) to find less expensive restaurants for entertaining clients.

3 The second suggestion that is made at the meeting is ...
   a) to increase the number of staff.
   b) to cut the number of staff.
   c) to give staff an easier workload and reduce stress.

Now read the next seven questions. Then listen again and mark your answers.

4 When Patricia responds to Jack's suggestion, she shows that ...
   a) she completely agrees.
   b) she doesn't agree.
   c) she doesn't have a strong opinion.

5 Patricia's opinion is:
   a) they will have bigger financial problems.
   b) they could lose customers.
   c) cheaper restaurants are a good idea.

6 In the conversation following Patricia's suggestion, it is clear that ...
   a) Jack and Patricia have exactly the same opinion.
   b) Jack and Patricia mostly agree.
   c) Jack and Patricia disagree completely.

7 Jack's opinion is:
   a) staff will not work hard if they are stressed and unhappy.
   b) job insecurity makes people work harder.
   c) it isn't necessary to dismiss anyone.

8 Max, the chairperson, ...
   a) agrees with Patricia.
   b) suggests that they look at other options.
   c) closes the meeting.

9 Maria …

  a) disagrees with Patricia.

  b) makes another suggestion.

  c) says she doesn't know enough about it.

10 Jack says: 'Are you saying that we need to … ?' He is …

  a) agreeing.

  b) disagreeing.

  c) clarifying the meaning.

Vocabulary

A **Mark the word that doesn't belong in each group.**

EXAMPLE:

  a) plane   **b)** train   **c)** car   **d)** ~~airport~~   **e)** truck

11 a) accountant **b)** solicitor **c)** stockbroker **d)** workaholic **e)** advertising executive

12 a) wages   **b)** bonus   **c)** promotion   **d)** pay   **e)** salary

13 a) worry   **b)** pressure   **c)** stress   **d)** flexitime **e)** rat race

14 a) people   **b)** product   **c)** promotion   **d)** price   **e)** place

15 a) boiled   **b)** bottled   **c)** fried   **d)** baked   **e)** grilled

B **Mark the verb that does <u>not</u> go with the noun.**

EXAMPLE:

  a) send   **b)** receive   **c)** pay   **d)** ~~make~~   an invoice

16 a) retain   **b)** entertain **c)** look after **d)** give up   customers

17 a) take up   **b)** re-arrange **c)** stick to   **d)** plan   a schedule

18 a) meet   **b)** miss   **c)** catch   **d)** keep within   a deadline

19 a) prepare   **b)** book   **c)** keep within **d)** discuss   the budget

20 a) implement **b)** increase   **c)** lose   **d)** forecast   sales

C **Choose the best word or phrase to fit the definition.**

21 A short description of a typical customer likely to be interested in a particular product.

  a) consumer profile   **b)** consumer behaviour

  c) consumer goods   **d)** consumer definition

22 An organisation's programme of advertising activities in order to sell a product.

  a) advertising figures   **b)** advertising executive

  c) advertising campaign   **d)** advertising agency

23 A name or design that goes with a product or group of products so that they can be easily recognised by customers.

  a) range   **b)** brand   **c)** launch   **d)** niche

24 A group of products in a particular part of the market.

  a) market research   **b)** market share

  c) market survey   **d)** market segment

25 The length of time during which a company expects to sell a particular product before it has to replace it with a more up-to-date product.

  a) product life cycle   **b)** product range

  c) product timetable   **d)** product forecast

26 When someone loses their job in a company because the job is no longer needed.

    a) strike action   **b)** resignation

    c) redundancy   **d)** job insecurity

27 A large business organisation that consists of several different companies that have joined together.

    a) a complex   **b)** a conglomerate

    c) a component   **d)** a composition

28 Changing the way a company is organised or financed.

    a) re-assessing   **b)** re-defining   **c)** re-building   **d)** restructuring

29 A sudden, large growth in business or sales.

    a) boom   **b)** bust   **c)** launch   **d)** rocket

30 To give a small additional amount of money to someone to thank them for their service.

    a) bill   **b)** tip   **c)** swap   **d)** check

Functions

A **Choose the best response from the box.**

31 I'd like you to meet my assistant, Gerald Dyke. ....

32 How's business? ....

33 Would you like me to show you round? ....

34 Can I get you a drink? ....

35 Do you mind if I smoke? ....

> **a)** We're doing very well at the moment.
>
> **b)** Please go ahead.
>
> **c)** Fine thanks. How are you?
>
> **d)** Pleased to meet you.
>
> **e)** Yes, I'd love to.
>
> **f)** No thanks, not at the moment.
>
> **g)** It's very kind of you, but I don't have much time. I have a train to catch.

B **The phrases below are all commonly used in meetings. Match the phrases with the functions.**

36 How about forming a study group? ....

37 How do you mean exactly? ....

38 A study group! That's an excellent idea! ....

39 Hold on a minute. ....

40 I really don't agree. Isn't it going to take a lot of time? ....

> **a)** clarifying
>
> **b)** interrupting
>
> **c)** giving an opinion
>
> **d)** making a suggestion
>
> **e)** agreeing
>
> **f)** disagreeing

Grammar

A **Multi-word verbs**

Choose the best word from the box to complete each sentence.

up	around	for	after
down	off	in	to	out

41 The sales staff invited us for dinner, but we had to turn .....
the invitation as our plane was leaving at 7 o'clock that evening.

42 The company entertained their new customers at a very expensive hotel
and ran ..... an enormous bill.

43 The strike at the airport means that people from abroad can't get here.
So we've had to call ..... the meeting.

44 You can use your credit card to pay ..... the dinner.

45 The company restaurant doesn't offer very exciting food. I think we
should take our customers ..... for a meal.

B **Past and present perfect tenses**
**Complete this extract from a presentation about share price. Write the verb in
the correct tense: past simple or present perfect.**

As you can see in the chart, our share price (increase) *increased*
steadily between 1998 and 2000. But in the spring of 2000, it (begin)
.... ⁴⁶ to fall, and since then, the price (be) .... ⁴⁷ in steep
decline. There are several reasons for this. One is the global economy.
As you know, world trade (grow) .... ⁴⁸ rapidly in 1998 and 1999. But
then (come) .... ⁴⁹ a dramatic fall in share prices, particularly in the
technology sector. As a result of this, we (see) .... ⁵⁰ a big drop in
investor confidence over the last few years.

C **Questions**
**Reorder the words to make correct questions. The answers to the questions
are given to help you.**

EXAMPLE: you / arrive / at the airport / when / did
When did you arrive at the airport?
Answer: At four o'clock.

51 you / often / at a restaurant / entertain / clients / do ....
Answer: Yes, we do.

52 customers / how many / do / in the USA / you / have ....
Answer: About 120.

53 you / interested / in our range of luxury goods / are ....
Answer: Yes, we are.

54 travelling / where / you / are / to ....
Answer: Morocco.

55 at the conference / meet / people from overseas / did / how many / you
....
Answer: Quite a lot!

D **Future plans**
Choose the right word or phrase from the box to complete the sentences.

| ~~going to~~ | visiting | meeting | expect |
| going | visit | meet | planning | hoping to |

EXAMPLE: As you can see from my schedule, I'm _going to_ be out of the office next Monday.

56 On Monday I'm .... a supplier company in Dublin.

57 Their sales manager is .... me at the airport at 10 a.m.

58 After that we're .... out to the company's factory just outside the town.

59 I'm .... see their new production facilities.

60 If everything looks OK, I .... to sign a deal with them the same day.

Reading   Read the article and answer the questions on the next page.

Three simple steps to a four-day week

Have you ever dreamed of having a long weekend every weekend? If so, now may be the time to turn that fantasy into a reality. How? By convincing your boss to let you cram five days
5 work into just four. It won't be easy. So, to help you out, here's a three-step guide.

Step 1: ....

Remind yourself of your company's key objectives. Remind yourself, too, of your own
10 role and responsibilities. Now think about how you could do a four-day week and still meet all those targets. Go for creative solutions. But never lose sight of the practicalities.

Step 2: ....

15 After listening to your well thought-out plans, your boss will probably have a couple of objections. The key to getting him or her on your side is to predict the objections and prepare counter arguments in advance. Here is some
20 advice on what to say when your boss makes objections:

'Customer service will suffer.'
I can train my customers to call me only when I'm in the office. And I can tell my colleagues
25 how to handle my customers' requirements if something comes up when I'm out.

'What if something urgent happens?'
I'll get a mobile, and a pager.

'Colleagues who depend on you won't be able to
30 function without you.'
I will brief them fully on what I am doing and how I am doing it.

'It will mean more work for others.'
I've devised a system to ensure that all my work
35 will be done on time, every time, so no one will have to carry any extra responsibilities.

'If I allow you to work a four-day week, I'll have to do it for everyone.'
Surveys indicate that workers who have flexible
40 hours are more loyal and more dedicated and take less sick leave. This could be a positive move for the company.

'It will cost us money.'
Reports prove that flexible workers contribute
45 up to a third more than regular workers. If anything, I will be more productive than ever.

Step 3: ....

Of course, it's not just what you say that matters, but also how you say it. To improve your
50 chances of winning over your boss, speak in a calm and controlled voice. Even if you feel like shouting or walking out, don't. Instead, quietly and confidently repeat why a four-day week would be good for you and the company. Show
55 that you understand your boss's point of view and stress that this is in his or her interests as well.

From the *Guardian*

The article gives three simple steps to a four-day week. Which of the phrases below matches each of the three steps?

61 Step 1: ....

62 Step 2: ....

63 Step 3: ....

    a) Be calm and confident.

    b) Research the background.

    c) Consider possible objections.

    d) Look for practical solutions to problems.

64 Your boss's objections may be that you will not be able to ...
(Mark <u>all</u> the points that are given in the article.)

    a) go on long business trips.

    b) keep a good standard of customer service.

    c) deal with important things immediately.

    d) help your colleagues when they have problems.

    e) go to all the meetings.

    f) take on extra work when other people are sick.

    g) do all the work that you are responsible for.

65 Which of these are positive arguments for a four-day week?
(Mark <u>all</u> the points that are given in the article.)

    People who can work flexible hours ...

    a) are more productive.

    b) don't stay with the company very long.

    c) are not ill so often.

    d) take advantage of the system by doing less work.

66 What does it mean if workers are 'loyal' (line 41)?

    a) They care about the company.

    b) They take a lot of interest in the work.

    c) They are ready to take on more responsibility.

    d) They want to do well in their careers.

You are responsible for organising an international meeting for the marketing managers from each of your company's subsidiaries worldwide (about 24 people). Write a letter that you can send to each of the marketing managers. Use the information about the meeting from the box. You should write about 60–80 words.

<u>Purpose of meeting:</u> To discuss international marketing strategy and co-ordinate the marketing activities in different countries.

<u>When?</u> Thursday 4 April–Friday 5 April

<u>Where?</u> Conference Suite, Four Towers Hotel, Toronto, Canada

<u>Practical information:</u> Participants arrive Wednesday. Accommodation at Four Towers Hotel on Wednesday and Thursday nights.

Peterson Enterprises
285 West Road
Peterborough PT3 8JY
United Kingdom

Telephone +44 (0) 1733 003623
Facsimile   +44 (0) 1733 001059
www.petersonent.com

Dear

I am writing to invite you to a meeting ...

Please confirm that you will be able to attend.

Yours sincerely

International Marketing Manager

Progress Test 3 (Units 9–12)

You are going to hear part of a meeting between Suzanne Dupont and Rob Clements, her senior manager. Rob has asked Suzanne to come into his office.

Read the first three questions. Then listen and mark your answers.

1 Rob Clements and Suzanne Dupont discuss …
   a) Suzanne's present job.
   b) her present salary.
   c) a new job.

2 It's the responsibility of the Lisbon manager to …
   a) increase profits.
   b) increase turnover.
   c) increase the number of staff.

3 The team is …
   a) all British.
   b) all Portuguese.
   c) a mix of British and Portuguese.

Now read the next three questions. Then listen and write down the number you hear.

4 The number of people in the Lisbon team is: ………… .

5 The job contract they discuss is for ………… years.

6 Rob offers Suzanne a ………… percent increase in salary.

Read the next two questions. Then listen and mark your answers.

7 What does the package of benefits include?
   (Tick all the benefits that Rob talks about.)
   a) free travel
   b) free accommodation
   c) eight weeks' annual leave
   d) company car
   e) profit-related bonus
   f) full pension plan

8 What would Suzanne like?
   (Tick all the things she says she would like.)
   a) a bigger increase in salary
   b) a bigger office
   c) more information about the situation in Portugal
   d) the chance to work in another country
   e) time to think
   f) to visit Portugal next week

Vocabulary

A **Choose a word from the box to complete the list of things you would like to have if you were setting up a new business.**

EXAMPLE: *government* grants

9 availability of .... staff
10 low bank .... rates
11 .... local economy
12 .... rents in the area where you want to set up
13 .... incentives offered by the regional government
14 good .... links

a)	plant
b)	skilled
c)	trade
d)	tax
e)	cheap
f)	~~government~~
g)	stable
h)	transport
i)	interest

B **Replace the underlined words in the text with a word that has the opposite meaning.**

Stuart Francis is a good *bad* negotiator.

During discussions, he is generally calm .... 15 and shows a lot of patience .... 16. One of his strengths .... 17 is that he tends to be creative .... 18 when handling conflict. His negotiating counterparts say that he is sympathetic .... 19 and friendly .... 20 in his relationships with them.

C **Choose a word from the box to complete the description of product qualities.**

a) high	**b)** hard	**c)** ~~best~~	**d)** long
e) well	**f)** low	**g)** poor	

This is one of the *best*-selling products in its range. And you can see why. It's 21 .... -designed, and made from 22 .... -quality materials, which we have specially chosen for their 23 .... -wearing and 24 .... -lasting characteristics. And for all that, it's an incredibly 25 .... -cost option.

Functions

A Choose the best word or phrase from the box to complete the product presentation.

> **a)** is ideal for   **b)** made of   **c)** is designed to   **d)** also has
> **e)** a very useful feature   **f)** weighs   **g)** comes in   **h)** another
> **i)** has several special features   **j)** ~~Let me tell you something about~~

Let me tell you something about our new laptop computer, the G11.
This is a powerful little machine, and with 30 gigabytes of memory, it offers tremendous capacity. It .... [26] , including a built-in MP3 player with excellent sound quality. It .... [27] a CD burner so that you can both download music and record it onto CD. The G11 .... [28] travelling as it is extremely lightweight and .... [29] only 1600 grams. This lap-top .... [30] be used anywhere: at the airport, on the plane or in your hotel room. .... [31] is the infra-red port, which means that, in certain locations, you can connect to the Web without any wires. As a special offer, we are giving away a useful carrying case which is .... [32] best quality leather, and .... [33] several different colours. .... [34] advantage is that it comes with the latest software already installed.

B Choose the best phrase from the box to complete each of the short conversations.

> **a)** Really?
> **b)** How about if
> **c)** How about you?
> **d)** Why don't we come back to that later?
> **e)** We've got a deal.
> **f)** What do you like to do in your spare time?
> **g)** I can see your point of view.
> **h)** It's very kind of you, but another time perhaps.

Conversation 1

Chris: This project has been very hard work, so I hope to get some more free time now that it's finishing.

George: .... [35]

Chris: I love to go skiing in the winter.

George: .... [36] I like skiing too. Where do you usually go?

Chris: Canada. It's beautiful there, and there are not too many people. .... [37] Where do you usually go?

George: I like Austria.

Conversation 2

Charlie: Delivery next week is no good to me at all. I must have delivery in two days, or the deal is off.

Bobby: .... [38] . You don't want to wait a week for the goods. .... [39] we could promise delivery in three days?

Charlie: Well, we could think about that. .... [40]

Conversation 3

Alex: OK, that's it. We agree to your proposal. .... [41]

Jo: Excellent! Now we can celebrate. I'd like to invite you to my favourite restaurant for dinner tonight. Can you come?

Alex: .... [42] . I have a plane to catch at 8 p.m.

Jo: That's a pity. Next time, then.

Grammar

A Choose a verb from the box to complete each sentence and write it in the correct form, active or passive.

produce	modify	launch
manufacture	~~have~~	look at promote
offer	distribute	

The very first step in the launch of a new product is when the Research Department *has* an idea. In the next step, the Marketing Department .... [43] it, and decides if they think it will sell. Sometimes, the Research Department .... [44] the design a little. Next, a prototype .... [45] to see if it works. Then maybe it .... [46] to a small number of customers on a trial basis. If everything looks OK, the new product .... [47] on a large scale. The marketing department .... [48] the product through an advertising campaign, and then it .... [49] onto the market. Large quantities of the product .... [50] to sales outlets all over the world.

B Antonio Cortez discusses the visit of some customers with his assistant, Pedro Mendes. Write the verbs in the correct tense.

Antonio Cortez:

Our visitors from Korea (come) *are coming* at 9 a.m. on Thursday. As soon as they (arrive) .... [51] , I want you to get everyone together in Conference Room A. Katarina Fischer and I are going to be a bit late, so while you (wait) .... [52] for us, you can offer our guests some coffee and make them feel welcome. If they (want) .... [53] to start the meeting, just explain the problem. Please don't start discussing anything important until Katarina and I (get) .... [54] there.

Now, I've arranged a tour of the factory, and it would be good if we can visit the new production facilities before we (go) .... [55] for lunch at 12.30. If we (be) .... [56] behind schedule, we can always postpone the factory tour until the afternoon. It wouldn't be a good idea to start the tour after midday. I think our guests would feel unhappy if they (have) .... [57] to rush. OK. Now what about the new brochures? Are they ready yet?

Pedro Mendes:

Well, no. I talked to Marketing this morning and they said that the brochures (be) .... [58] delayed. They asked me when we (want) .... [59] to have them, and I said that we (need) .... [60] to have them for Thursday morning.

Writing

You are one of the group from Korea who visited Antonio and Pedro (see Grammar Exercise B). Following your visit, you write a letter of thanks to Antonio.

In your letter, you can talk about:

- a successful meeting
- meeting Katarina Fischer and Pedro Mendes
- an interesting tour of the factory
- lunch
- doing business in the future.

155-8 Yeonhee-Dong, Seoul 120-100 Korea

Geo-D

Dear Antonio

I am writing to thank you ...

Reading

Read the article about starting your own business. Some words have been taken out of the text. These words are listed (a to g) in the box on page 27. Complete each gap with the correct word.

Have you got what it takes to start your own business?

How do you really make it happen? How do you raise the .... [61]? Is there anywhere you can go for help?

Chidi Ngwaba says funding a business yourself with savings is 'a bit like having a baby. I feel like we're living a dream.'

Their .... [62] was to open a place selling healthy fresh-cooked, vegetarian food. Neither Chidi nor his wife, Uchenna, has any experience of food, other than eating it. Their cash has stretched to employing a team of people to run their company, Plant, and they hope to have three more outlets by the end of the year. The Ngwabas believe they have no direct competition. 'I think it's something new,' Ms Ngwaba says confidently. If things don't work out, they'll sell their house and move in with their parents.

The need to feel safe and the fear of .... [63] can often stop people taking their first steps towards starting up a business. But according to Simon Woodroffe, founder of the restaurant chain YO! Sushi, it is the fear of not following your dream which moves people. It is better to try and fail than never to have tried, he believes. When I ask him whether now is a difficult time to start a business, Mr Woodroffe says: 'It's always the right time to .... [64] a business.' With YO! Sushi now quite stable, Mr Woodroffe is starting new ventures. YOTEL! and Body YO! are coming soon.

Similarly motivated is Mark Blandford, founder of online agency Sportingbet. Sportingbet went live in October 1998, with no customers and no turnover. Today he says: 'We're a profitable dot.com.' His expected .... [65] this year is £927 million.

And his advice for would-be entrepreneurs? 'Have a vision, spot a new niche and be sufficiently convinced to go for it 100%.' It's not the advice a bank would offer. A banker's advice would centre more on researching your idea and on drawing up detailed business plans. You probably need both to get started.

From the *Guardian*

> **a)** dream
> **b)** customers
> **c)** money
> **d)** turnover
> **e)** failure
> **f)** business
> **g)** start

Choose the best answer.

66 Chidi and Uchenna Ngwaba ...

    a) borrowed money from the bank to fund their business.

    b) already run three restaurants.

    c) run Plant completely on their own.

    d) are not afraid of competitors.

67 Simon Woodroffe ...

    a) owns a number of restaurants.

    b) thinks that it is not a good time for starting a business now.

    c) has a business which is not doing well.

    d) does not plan to expand his business any more.

68 Mark Blandford ...

    a) has a business with a turnover that exceeds £1 billion.

    b) started without customers.

    c) nearly went out of business in 1998.

    d) offers the same advice that a banker would offer.

69 To 'have a vision' (line 39) means to ...

    a) have good support.

    b) have imagination and a clear purpose.

    c) have good eyesight.

    d) have good sense and be practical.

70 To 'spot a new niche' (line 39) means to ...

    a) copy what other entrepreneurs are doing.

    b) create a new product.

    c) find a good location for your business.

    d) see an opening in the market.

Exit Test

Listening You are going to hear a telephone conversation between Philippe Charpentier and An Mei Tan. An Mei Tan calls from Singapore to finalise the arrangements for Philippe's visit there in two weeks.

Listen and fit the activities below into the timetable. Write the number of the activity in the correct place in the timetable. The first one has been done as an example.

	Monday	Tuesday	Wednesday	Thursday	Friday	Saturday	Sunday
morning							
afternoon	0						
evening							
night							

- **0)** Arrive in Singapore
- **1** Visit Asian Trading Corporation
- **2** Travel to Kuala Lumpur
- **3** Meet Mr Makhoub
- **4** Leave for Jakarta
- **5** Return to Paris
- **6** Which of the tasks below have not been done yet? Tick the boxes in column 1.
- **7** Which tasks are Philippe's responsibility? Tick the boxes in column 2.

Listen again and tick the boxes. One answer is marked for you as an example.

	Things not yet done	Things Philippe must do
a) e-mail the flight numbers	✓	✓
b) arrange the meeting at the Import Office		
c) confirm the meeting with Mr Chong		
d) make sure the samples are ready		
e) collect the samples from Production		
f) finalise the meetings in Jakarta		

Vocabulary

A Word families

In the report below, there is one wrong word on each line. Write the correct form of the word on the line on the right. The first one has been done as an example.

Unfortunately, I have to report that the launch of the Firecrest has been a <u>fail</u>.	*failure*
This is partly because of difficult economical conditions at the present time.	8 ....
However, it is also because we were not able to meet the safe standards	9 ....
that the market demands at present. Our competitives, on the other hand,	10 ....
have been much more success with their product, the Gold Rush.	11 ....
They have also found better solvings to technical questions	12 ....
leading to better reliableness.	13 ....

B Complete the text by writing one appropriate word in each gap.

If you want to *achieve* success with a new product, there are a number of steps you have to get right. First, you should identify a .... [14] in the market: a need for a product that doesn't exist yet. Then you can either .... [15] a completely new product idea, or modify an existing product idea. It is important to .... [16] market research to check if your idea will have a market, and to be able to target the right .... [17] . Next, you must decide how to .... [18] the product, for example by developing an effective advertising campaign.

C Complete the sentences by writing an appropriate word in each gap.

19 All the people who work for a company or in a country are called its labour ....

20 Balance of .... means the difference in value between the goods and services that are exported and imported.

21 The euro, US dollar and pound sterling are all examples of ....

22 A company which sells direct to the public rather than to shops is known as a ....

23 A method of buying where the customer chooses goods at home, from the Internet for example, and asks for the goods to be sent by post: .... order.

24 A person who puts money into a business, either directly or by buying shares, for example, is called an ....

25 A date or time by which you have to do something or complete something is a ....

26 A company that is at least half-owned by another company is called a ....

27 Time that you spend working in your job in addition to your normal working hours is called ....

28 When you have passed examinations at school, university or in your profession that make you suitable for a job, we say that you are ....

Grammar

A **Choose the best word or phrase to complete the e-mail below.**

Dear Frank

Thanks *for* your e-mail. I apologise .... [29] not contacting you before.
We .... [30] for a reply .... [31] our latest proposal to Lex
Corporation. Unfortunately, they .... [32] about the length of the
service contract. But we are hoping .... [33] this problem soon. If they
.... [34] to our offer, we will be able to sign the contract .... [35] the
end of this week.

I believe that all the documents .... [36] to you a week .... [37] .
.... [38] you please confirm that you have received them? I will let you
know as soon as possible when we can go ahead.

Best regards

Anton

EXAMPLE: **a)** to   **b)** ~~for~~   **c)** of   **d)** about

29	**a)** to	**b)** in	**c)** that	**d)** for
30	**a)** still wait	**b)** waited still	**c)** have waited	**d)** are still waiting
31	**a)** to	**b)** of	**c)** at	**d)** on
32	**a)** don't agree	**b)** are not agree	**c)** are not agreeing	**d)** were not agreeing
33	**a)** for solving	**b)** to solve	**c)** that we solve	**d)** we are solving
34	**a)** will agree	**b)** are agreeing	**c)** agree	**d)** agreed
35	**a)** in	**b)** till	**c)** by	**d)** to
36	**a)** sent	**b)** are sending	**c)** are sent	**d)** were sent
37	**a)** past	**b)** later	**c)** ago	**d)** since
38	**a)** Should	**b)** May	**c)** Can	**d)** Do

B **In the report on a meeting, which you can read below, there is one extra word
on each line. Cross out the extra word so that the text is correct.**

EXAMPLE: The question of personal expenses was raised ~~up~~.

39 Several people have overspent their allowances last year, and the

40 finance manager asked to everybody to try to reduce spending. However,

41 some people felt that the maximum of allowance was too low. It was suggested

42 that allowances should to be increased by 5 to 10 percent. This increase in staff

43 allowances could be included in to the budget for the next quarter.

Functions

A **Choose the best response from the box.**

EXAMPLE: Thanks for showing me round. *b)*

44 Would you like to join us for dinner this evening?	**a)** Thanks, but I've already booked a taxi.
45 How about a coffee?	**b)** ~~Not at all. It was my pleasure~~.
46 What do you recommend?	**c)** I'm glad you enjoyed it.
47 Can I offer you a lift to the station?	**d)** I don't mind.
48 Well, goodbye. All the best.	**e)** It's very kind of you, but I already have an engagement for this evening.
49 Thanks for the meal. It was delicious!	**f)** That's all right.
50 I'm sorry I'm a bit late.	**g)** Not just at the moment, thanks.
	h) I'll be in touch soon.
	i) Yes.
	j) The fish is very good here.

B **Complete this dialogue from a meeting with appropriate phrases from the box.**

a) Excellent idea!	**b)** I think it would be better to
c) ~~Let's move on to~~	**d)** I think I agree with you.
e) We could	**f)** Do we all agree?
g) Can I have some suggestions?	**h)** I have another suggestion.
i) I'm not sure I agree.	

Chair: OK. *Let's move on to* the next point on the agenda. How are we going to entertain our Italian delegates at the weekend? 51

Anka: .... 52 take them to see a historic site: Stonehenge, for example.

Boris: .... 53 I'm sure they would enjoy that.

Carol: .... 54 Why don't we take them motor racing? There's a track at Castle Combe. We can check if there's a race next Saturday.

Anka: .... 55 Not everybody likes motor racing.

Boris: And what if we have bad weather? .... 56 go to a town, like Oxford or Stratford. Then we can visit museums if it's raining.

Anka: .... 57 Oxford would be interesting. And then we can find a nice restaurant to have lunch.

Chair: 58

All: Yes.

Chair: OK then. Let's arrange a trip to Oxford.

Read the article and then answer the questions below.

Saint Laurent wraps up haute couture career

Yves Saint Laurent, the French designer, signalled the end of an era in fashion when he announced his retirement from haute couture at an emotional press conference at
5 his Paris salon.

'At the age of 18, I had the luck to become Christian Dior's assistant, to succeed him at 21 and to be successful from my first show in 1958. Since then I have lived for my work,' he
10 said. 'However, today I have chosen to say farewell to the profession that I have so loved.'

The quiet 65-year-old said that this month's collection at Paris's Centre Georges
15 Pompidou would look back at his past work, and would be the last show of his career. With his long-time friend and business partner Pierre Berge at his side, Saint Laurent looked pale and unwell, but elegant
20 in a black suit and white shirt as he told journalists that the YSL haute couture collection would close with his retirement.

He thanked François Pinault, the French entrepreneur who has bankrolled Saint
25 Laurent's loss-making haute couture since 1999.

'I tell myself that I created the wardrobe of the modern woman, that I took part in a major change in fashion during the second
30 half of the twentieth century. I did it with clothes, which is of course less important than music, architecture, painting and many other arts, but even so I did it.'

After standing for applause, Saint
35 Laurent took no questions and left the room for Mr Berge to explain his decision.

'Yves Saint Laurent feels less and less at ease in a fashion industry in which haute couture exists only in name,' Mr Berge said.
40 'The era of haute couture is over. We live now in a time of jeans and Nike. Saint Laurent has no competitors any more and it is no fun playing a game of tennis on one's own.'

45 Mr Berge denied reports that Mr Pinault had decided to wind up the operation for financial reasons. 'Haute couture businesses typically make losses, and our losses are less than expected,' Mr Berge said.

From *The Financial Times*

Choose the best answer.

59 This newspaper article reports ...
  a) that Yves Saint Laurent is thinking of retiring.
  b) that Yves Saint Laurent has decided to retire.
  c) the official announcement of Yves Saint Laurent's retirement.
  d) public reaction to Yves Saint Laurent's retirement.

60 Mr Berge said that Yves Saint Laurent retired because ...
  a) he had sold his business.
  b) he wanted to live abroad.
  c) there was no place for haute couture in the modern world.
  d) he had reached 65 years of age.

61 Yves Saint Laurent said that his career success ...
  a) began to develop when he was thirty years old.
  b) was due to good luck in his early years.
  c) was due to hard work.
  d) was due to the fact that he had no competition.

62 His last show at the Pompidou Centre was designed to …
- **a)** be artistic and creative.
- **b)** be the best of his whole career.
- **c)** show designs from his whole career.
- **d)** show mainly informal clothes.

63 Yves Saint Laurent said that …
- **a)** clothes are as important as architecture.
- **b)** he was also interested in furniture.
- **c)** he was happy with the current trends in the industry.
- **d)** he was proud that his work made a big impact on fashion in the last century.

64 Yves Saint Laurent …
- **a)** looked strong and healthy.
- **b)** answered lots of questions.
- **c)** didn't say anything about his reasons for closing his business.
- **d)** stayed in his seat until the end of the conference.

65 'Wraps up' (in the headline) means …
- **a)** continues.
- **b)** regrets.
- **c)** develops.
- **d)** ends.

66 To 'bankroll' (line 24) means …
- **a)** to give funding.
- **b)** to give financial advice.
- **c)** to act as a financial manager.
- **d)** to negotiate with the banks.

67 'Feels less and less at ease' (line 37) means …
- **a)** finds the work more difficult.
- **b)** is increasingly uncomfortable.
- **c)** feels more and more tired.
- **d)** feels more and more angry.

Writing

You are a personnel manager. Your company's administrative offices are open-plan with 60 people working in the same large space.

You have been asked to carry out a survey of employee opinions about office space and working conditions. The results of your survey are given below.

Complete the short memo, giving your report on the survey. Describe the results, and make recommendations. You should write between 150 and 200 words.

Survey: 60 questionnaires sent to office staff. 56 returned.

Results:

	Yes	No	Don't know
Do you think that the company offices are too small?	92%	2%	6%
Do you think you have enough personal work space?	37%	62%	1%
Do you think that an open-plan office reduces efficiency?	58%	25%	17%

What are the main problems of the present arrangement?

Noise	96%
Not enough space	72%
Too many interruptions	49%

What are the advantages?

Easy communication	64%
Friendly atmosphere	55%

	Yes	No	Don't know
Would you prefer to share a small office with 2 or 3 other people?	66%	18%	16%

Recommend:
1) Try to find additional office space.
2) Change from open-plan office to small offices.

Memo

To: Karl Beloff, Administrative Director
From: .... ,
Date: Personnel Manager
Subject: Survey on office working conditions

I was asked to carry out a survey of employees' opinions about the current working conditions in our administrative offices. In this memo, I present the results of this survey.

Survey
A questionnaire ...

A copy of this questionnaire is attached.

Results
The results from the questionnaire show ...

Recommendations
Based on the results of this survey, I recommend: ...

Speaking Test

You are going to have a five-minute oral test. You should prepare your answers to the questions before starting the test. You will have five minutes to prepare.

1   Your examiner will ask you some general questions about yourself, your occupation and your future plans.

2   You will then be asked some questions about two companies which are described below. Use the information in the chart to give your answers.

	Amazon	Arcadia
Head Office:	Seattle, USA	London, UK
Activity:	retails books, music, DVDs, videos, etc. via the Internet	retails clothes through stores, mail order catalogues and via the Internet
Turnover last year:	$2.76 billion	£1.89 billion
Profit:	minus $1.41 billion	minus £66.6 million
Number of employees:	9,000	22,066

3   Imagine you would like to work in online selling. Which of the two companies above would you prefer to work for? Give one or two reasons.

Answer Key

Entry Test

Listening

1 b
2 b
3 c
4 b
5 b
6 b
7 c
8 a
9 c
10 a

Vocabulary

A		B		C		D	
11	d	16	f	21	a	26	b
12	b	17	a	22	d	27	d
13	e	18	d	23	c	28	c
14	a	19	h	24	b	29	a
15	a	20	g	25	d	30	c

Grammar

A		B	
31	b	36	spent
32	c	37	cost
33	a	38	worked
34	e	39	made
35	g	40	learned / learnt

C		D	
41	c	51	How many people do work for your company?
42	b	52	Is it is a manufacturing company?
43	a	53	Do can you describe some of your products?
44	b	54	Are these products are yours?
45	d	55	Where to do you export to?
46	c		
47	b		
48	c		
49	d		
50	c		

Reading

56 a
57 d
58 a
59 b
60 a
61 a
62 c
63 b
64 a
65 d

1 mark for each correct answer = 65 marks

Progress Test 1

Listening

1 b
2 d
3 a
4 Brazil
5 1969
6 c
7 $2.8 billion
8 $353 million
9 (more than) 10,000
10 a

Vocabulary

A		B		C			
11	d	16	c	21	d	26	d
12	b	17	f	22	b	27	c
13	a	18	a	23	a	28	b
14	e	19	h	24	b	29	d
15	d	20	e	25	c	30	b

Functions

31 c
32 a
33 d
34 d
35 c

Grammar

A		B			
36	is growing	44	had	52	told
37	employ	45	was trying	53	was having
38	are recruiting	46	demanded	54	wanted
39	produce	47	didn't have	55	praised
40	are developing	48	telephoned		
41	know	49	could		
42	like	50	was losing		
43	are launching	51	rang		

C	
56	f
57	a
58	b
59	d
60	c

Reading

61 c
62 a
63 b
64 c
65 c
66 a
67 a
68 c
69 b
70 b

One mark for each correct answer = 70 marks

Writing Task: 10 marks

Award marks as follows:

1	clarity:	4	(Are the sentences clear? Is the text easy to read and understand?)
2	accuracy:	4	(Deduct half a mark for each major grammatical mistake.)
3	content:	2	(If all the key points are included.)

Overall total: 80 marks

Progress Test 2

Listening

1 a
2 c
3 b
4 b
5 b
6 c
7 a
8 b
9 c
10 c

Vocabulary

A	11	d	B	16	d	C	21	a		26	c
	12	c		17	a		22	c		27	b
	13	d		18	c		23	b		28	d
	14	a		19	b		24	d		29	a
	15	b		20	a		25	a		30	b

Functions

A	31	d	B	36	d
	32	a		37	a
	33	g		38	e
	34	f		39	b
	35	b		40	f

Grammar

A	41	down	B	46	began
	42	up		47	has been
	43	off		48	grew
	44	for		49	came
	45	out		50	have seen

C
51 Do you often entertain clients at a restaurant?
52 How many customers do you have in the USA?
53 Are you interested in our range of luxury goods?
54 Where are you travelling to?
55 How many people from overseas did you meet at the conference?

D 56 visiting
57 meeting
58 going
59 hoping to
60 expect

One mark for each correct answer = 60 marks

Reading

61 d
62 c
63 a
64 b, c, d, g (one mark for each correct answer)
65 a, c (one mark for each correct answer)
66 a

10 marks for this section

Writing Task: 10 marks

Award marks as follows:

1	clarity:	4	(Are the sentences clear? Is the text easy to read and understand?)
2	accuracy:	4	(Deduct half a mark for each major grammatical mistake.)
3	appropriacy:	2	(If the language is polite and suitable for a letter.)

Overall total: 80 marks

Progress Test 3

Listening

1 c
2 a
3 b
4 6 (six)
5 3 (three)
6 30
7 b, d, e (Give one mark if all correct; deduct half a mark for each mistake.)
8 a, c, e (Give one mark if all correct; deduct half a mark for each mistake.)

Vocabulary

A	9	b	B	15	nervous / emotional	C	21	e well-designed
	10	i		16	impatience		22	a high-quality
	11	g		17	weaknesses		23	b hard-wearing
	12	e		18	uncreative		24	d long-lasting
	13	d		19	unsympathetic		25	f low-cost
	14	h		20	unfriendly			

Functions

A	26	i	B	35	f
	27	d		36	a
	28	a		37	c
	29	f		38	g
	30	c		39	b
	31	e		40	d
	32	b		41	e
	33	g		42	h
	34	h			

Grammar

A	43	looks at	B	51	arrive
	44	modifies		52	are waiting
	45	is produced / is manufactured		53	want
	46	is offered		54	get
	47	is manufactured / is produced		55	go
	48	promotes		56	are
	49	is launched		57	had
	50	are distributed		58	would be
				59	wanted
				60	needed

Reading

61 c
62 a
63 e
64 g
65 d
66 d
67 a
68 b
69 b
70 d

One mark for each correct answer = 70 marks

Writing task: 10 marks

Award marks as follows:

1 clarity: 4 (Are the sentences clear? Is the text easy to read and understand?)

2 accuracy: 4 (Deduct half a mark for each major grammatical mistake.)

3 appropriacy: 2 (If the language is polite and suitable for a letter.)

Overall total: 80 marks

Exit Test

Listening

	M	T	W	Th	F	S	S
morning		(1)	(2)	(4)			
afternoon			(3)				
evening							
night							(5)

	Things not yet done	Things Philippe must do
a) e-mail the flight numbers		
b) arrange the meeting at the Import Office		
c) confirm the meeting with Mr Chong	✓	
d) make sure the samples are ready		
e) collect the samples from Production	✓	✓
f) finalise the meetings in Jakarta	✓	

For 6 and 7 score one mark for each correct tick.

Total marks for listening: 9

Vocabulary

A **8** economic
9 safety
10 competitors
11 successful
12 solutions
13 reliability

B **(Accept any of the answers given below.)**
14 gap/niche/opening

15 invent/create/develop/design
16 do/carry out
17 market/customers/group
18 promote/advertise/market/launch

C **19** force
20 trade
21 currency/currencies
22 retailer/retail company
23 mail
24 investor
25 deadline
26 subsidiary
27 overtime
28 qualified

One mark for each correct answer = 21 marks

Grammar

A **29** d
30 d
31 a
32 a
33 b
34 c
35 c
36 d
37 c
38 c

B **39** Several people ~~have~~ overspent their allowances last year, and the
40 finance manager asked ~~to~~ everybody to try to reduce spending, However,
41 some people felt that the maximum ~~of~~ allowance was too low. it was suggested
42 that allowances should ~~to~~ be increased by 5 to 10 per cent. This increase in staff
43 allowances could be included in ~~to~~ the budget for the next quarter.

One mark for each correct answer = 15 marks

Functions

A **44** e
45 g
46 j
47 a
48 h
49 c
50 f

B **51** g
52 e
53 a
54 h
55 i
56 b
57 d
58 f

One mark for each correct answer = 9 marks

Reading

59 c
60 c
61 b
62 c
63 d
64 c
65 d
66 a
67 b

One mark for each correct answer = 9 marks

Writing task: 11 marks

Award marks as follows:

1. clarity: 4 (Are the sentences clear? Is the text easy to read and understand?)
2. accuracy: 4 (Deduct half a mark for each major grammatical mistake.)
3. content: 3 (If all the key facts are included.)

Overall total: 80 marks

Audio Scripts

Entry Test

Ruth: Excuse me. Are you Irena Gavare? (Pron: GUV-AR-AY)
Irena: Yes, that's right.
Ruth: Hello. I'm Ruth Simonds. Welcome to Luton!
Irena: It's nice to meet you, Mrs Simonds.
Ruth: Can I introduce my assistant, Bob Postgate?
Bob: Hello. Good to meet you.
Irena: Good to meet you too.
Bob: We got your message this morning that your flight was delayed. I'm sorry you had such a terrible journey!
Irena: Oh, it wasn't so bad. It was because of the very cold temperatures in Latvia. The plane couldn't take off! I'm sorry to be so late!
Ruth: It's no problem for us! I'm just glad you're here! Let's go up to my office. We're on the fifth floor, so we'll take the lift. It's this way.
Irena: Oh!
Bob: Can I help you with your luggage?
Irena: Oh, thank you!

Progress Test 1

Nelson Ferreira:
OK, so before I tell you about our exciting new model, let me first give you a few basic facts about our company.
Did you know that we are one of the largest aircraft manufacturers in the world? And that we make commercial aircraft, as well as military planes, and of course corporate aircraft?
We were set up in 1969 by the government of Brazil. And we were based then – as we are today – in São José dos Campos, in Brazil. Here you can see a picture of our factories.
The next milestone in our company history was in 1994. In that year we were privatised – which meant that our shares could be traded on the stock exchange. In fact, today we are listed on both the New York and São Paulo stock exchanges. This gave us the opportunity to raise finance for new ideas.
Now let me show you some figures.
Our revenues – as you can see – have increased steadily every year since 1996. Last year we reached a gross revenue of two point eight billion US dollars – which gave us net earnings of three hundred and fifty-three million dollars.
And the number of employees has also increased from three thousand eight hundred, five years ago, to more than ten thousand today. So you can see that we have grown very rapidly since our privatisation, and we are still growing.
OK. So that was a very short background to the company. Now I'll move on to the main point which is of interest to you: our new executive jet plane – which we call Ambassador. This is the latest in our range of corporate aircraft and it has already attracted a great deal of attention … [FADE]

Progress Test 2

Max: OK, everybody. As you know, the costs of running this unit have increased dramatically in the last year, and we have to find some way to cut down our expenses. I'd like to get your ideas. Jack – what do you think?

Jack: Well, a big part of our budget is spent on entertaining clients. Er we always use the most expensive restaurants for this. I think we could look for restaurants that would offer a better deal.
Max: Yes. Patricia?
Patricia: That's really not a good idea! Do you want our clients to know that we have financial problems? They're going to notice if we start taking them out to cheap restaurants – and they're going to take their business somewhere else!
Jack: I didn't mean *cheap* restaurants! I meant restaurants that offer better value for money. They can still be *good* restaurants.
Max: OK – I think the savings there will not be very great. But let's make a note about entertainment costs. We can come back to that point later. What other suggestions do you have? Patricia?
Patricia: Well, I know I'm not going to be popular for saying this, but I think we have too many staff here. Some people have a very easy workload.
Jack: Are you saying that we need to cut staff?
Patricia: That's exactly what I'm saying. We could reduce the number by 2 or 3 and still be just as efficient. More efficient probably!
Jack: I think that would have a very bad effect on everybody. People will start to be afraid of losing their jobs. They'll be stressed and unhappy and then they won't work so hard!
Patricia: I don't agree. I think a little job insecurity makes people work harder! Nobody wants to be the next one to go.
Max: Well, I don't think anybody should have to lose their job. Our problems aren't that big yet! Let's consider some other options. I'm sure we can find some easier solutions. Maria – you've been very quiet. You must have some suggestions?
Maria: Well … I'm new in this unit, and I don't know the situation very well yet …

Progress Test 3

Rob: Come in, Suzanne. Have a seat.
Suzanne: Thanks.
Rob: The reason I asked you to come and see me is, erm – we are thinking of offering you a new position.
Suzanne: A new position?
Rob: Yes. The manager of our Lisbon office is leaving. We're looking for someone with the right skills and abilities to take up his position. We think you're the right person for the job.
Suzanne: Lisbon! That sounds exciting! But what is the job exactly?
Rob: Well, you'd be in charge of the Portuguese business unit. One of your tasks would be to make it more profitable than it is at the moment. It would be a big challenge. You'd be responsible for a team of six Portuguese staff and you would have to develop good relationships with them and win their trust. You will need to be very committed. We think the new manager should be ready to stay in Lisbon for at least three years.

Suzanne:	Yes, I see.
Rob:	Have a look at these facts and figures … [FADE]
Suzanne:	… [FADE back in] And can I ask about salary?
Rob:	We would offer you a thirty percent increase on your present salary.
Suzanne:	Hmm. A thirty percent increase is not very much for such a challenging job. Especially as I would have to adapt to living in a new country.
Rob:	It's just part of the package. We would also pay your rent on a good apartment. You'd have a company car, and a bonus that will increase with the profit that the unit makes.
Suzanne:	That's fine if the unit makes a profit!
Rob:	It will be your job to ensure that it makes a profit.
Suzanne:	Well, I need time to think. And I would like to find out more about the job, and about the situation in Portugal.
Rob:	Of course you would. You don't have to decide now. If you're interested, I could arrange for you to visit the Lisbon office so that you can have a look.
Suzanne:	That would be great!

Exit Test

Philippe:	Hello. Philippe Charpentier speaking.
An Mei Tan	Hello Philippe. This is An Mei Tan calling from Singapore. How are you?
Phil:	Fine thanks. How are you?
An Mei:	Very well, thank you. Philippe, I'm calling you about your trip over to Singapore in two weeks' time. I need to check what time you are arriving.
Phil:	Let me see … Yes, here we are – I arrive on Monday 4th March at three in the afternoon.
An Mei:	OK, that's good. I will be at the airport to meet you and take you to your hotel.
Phil:	Thank you very much.
An Mei:	But can you please e-mail me with your flight numbers?
Phil:	Of course. I'll do it right away.
An Mei:	Now, I have arranged three meetings while you are in Singapore. One is with the Asian Trading Corporation – that's on Tuesday morning. Then, you will visit the Import Office on Tuesday afternoon. Oh – and do you think you will be able to meet Mr Chong on Monday evening? Will you be very tired after your long flight?
Phil:	Oh no, I don't think so. That will be all right.
An Mei:	OK, then I will confirm that meeting for Monday at seven p.m. And you leave for Kuala Lumpur on Wednesday – is that right?
Phil:	Yes – at eight-thirty in the morning.
An Mei:	Good. Because I've arranged for you to meet Mr Ali Makhoub in Kuala Lumpur at two p.m. the same day. Will that be OK for you?
Phil:	Yes, fine.
An Mei:	Do you have all the samples ready to bring with you, because Mr Makhoub is very interested in seeing them?
Phil:	Oh, yes. They're ready – I checked them yesterday. I just have to collect them from the Production people.
An Mei:	Oh, good. And your flight on to Jakarta, when is that?
Phil:	On Thursday. In the morning.
An Mei:	Right. I have to apologise because I haven't yet set up any meetings for you in Jakarta. I've had some problems contacting Mr Sankaran. But I hope I will get everything fixed in the next couple of days.
Phil:	That's fine. We still have two weeks.
An Mei:	And have you booked your flight back to Paris?

| Phil: | Yes – it's on Sunday the tenth leaving at 10 o'clock at night. I decided to stay over the weekend as I haven't been to Jakarta before. I thought it would be nice to look around, do some sightseeing … [FADE] |

Model Answers to Writing Tasks

Entry Test

There is no writing task in the Entry Test.

Progress Test 1

We have looked at several models of aircraft which could be suitable for our company and we would like to recommend the Ambassador, which is manufactured in Brazil by BrazAir Corporation.

This aircraft has several advantages ...

The performance of this aircraft is excellent. It is a large size and is extremely comfortable. It is reliable and safe. BrazAir also offers a good after-sales service contract. This model is medium-priced and has low running costs, so we think it is the best solution to meet the company's needs.

We attach a detailed report.

Progress Test 2

Dear ....

I am writing to invite you to a meeting for all marketing managers from each subsidiary worldwide. The purpose of the meeting is to discuss international marketing strategy and co-ordinate the marketing activities in different countries.

The meeting will take place on 4 and 5 April at the conference suite of the Four Towers Hotel in Toronto, Canada.

Please arrange your flights to arrive on Wednesday, 3 April. Accommodation will be reserved for you on Wednesday and Thursday nights.

Please confirm that you will be able to attend.

Yours sincerely,

International Marketing Manager

Progress Test 3

Dear Antonio

I am writing to thank you for your hospitality last Thursday. It was a very successful meeting and we were pleased to meet Katarina Fischer and Pedro Mendes.

We were very interested to see your new production facilities. Many thanks for showing us around. We also enjoyed the delicious lunch.

Please give our best wishes to Katarina and Pedro. We look forward to doing business with you in the future.

Yours sincerely

Exit Test

I was asked to carry out a survey of employees' opinions about the current working conditions in our administrative offices. In this memo, I present the results of this survey.

Survey
A questionnaire was sent to 60 employees. 56 people returned it.
A copy of this questionnaire is attached.

Results
The results from the questionnaire show that most employees (92 percent) think that the company offices are too small. Nearly two-thirds (62 percent) say they do not have enough personal work space. Just over half (58 percent) think that an open-plan office reduces efficiency. The main problems which people described were: noise, not enough space and too many interruptions.
However, the advantages are: easy communication and a friendly atmosphere. When asked if they would prefer to share a small office with two or three people, two-thirds of employees (66 percent) said yes; 18 percent said no; and 16 percent didn't know.

Recommendations
Based on the results of this survey, I recommend:
    1) trying to find additional office space.
    2) changing from open-plan to small offices.

Exit Test: Speaking

Examiner's Notes

The oral test should take only about five minutes. You should give each candidate about five minutes to prepare the questions before starting the test.

1   Ask the candidate some general questions about himself/herself.
    e.g. What do you do?
    What do you enjoy most about your job/occupation?
    What did you do before that?
    What are your plans for the future?

2   Ask the candidate specific questions about the information in the table.
    e.g. Where is Amazon's head office located?
    What do they sell? How do they sell?
    What was their turnover last year?
    How many employees do they have?

3   Ask the candidate to say which company they would prefer to work for. If he/she does not give reasons, ask why they would choose this company.

Marking the speaking test:

15 marks

Award for:

2 – understanding the questions
3 – communicating ideas without the need for the examiner to clarify meaning
2 – reasonable accuracy in the use of different tenses
2 – accuracy in expressing numbers
2 – expanding on answers (not just giving a minimal response)
2 – speaking without too much hesitation
2 – clarity of pronunciation